Chaos Has A Name

Lauren Tormey

BookLeaf Publishing

India | USA | UK

Presentation by *BookLeaf Publishing*

Web: www.bookleafpub.com

E-mail: info@bookleafpub.com

ISBN: 9789357613101

First edition 2023

PREFACE

This book is a declaration of freedom from my mind, as well as an apology for the chaos I have created.

I am sorry to everyone, for being the bomb.

Chaos has a Name

Chaos is wildfire, fighting fire;

engulfing everything in its furry;

giving Carbon Monoxide kisses goodbye.

Chaos is the firework fuse,;

triggering a lightshow of explosion;

artfully willing a spectacular blackout.

Chaos is a capricious grenade;

itching to be mishandled;

blindly begging anyone to pull the pin.

Chaos is an impartial plague;

undoubtedly lurking in the shadows;

taking names for the sake of self-preservation.

Chaos has a name,
has a body,
has a soul?

Chaos has a name;
Chaos is my name.

Brother

My eyes follow you from room to room.

Prayers unanswered; shadows loom.

My heart grieves red: impending doom.

I check your breathing tune to tune.

Tenacious as you rise; false truth.

My eyes follow you from room to room.

Jolted awake at ten past two.

A smile forms; slapping curtains move.

My heart grieves red: impending doom.

I see your face and my insides swoon.

Calm breathing ceases; fear resumes.

My eyes follow you from room to room.

I fear that death is coming soon.

Tests untrusted; thoughts consumed.

My heart grieves red: impending doom.

I plead before the stars and moon.

Cries echo silent; malignant gloom.

My eyes follow you from room to room.

My heart grieves red: impending doom.

His Hands

I had a dream about you the other night.

We were so happy.

Your arms outstretched to hug me--

followed by your hands.

The strong hands I used to grasp in the ocean.

me-- much too young to be out so far.

You-- my shield.

The waves crashing;

salt spraying in my face.

my reckless spirit free in the vastness

of n e v e r- e n d i n g,

calm.

Your hands are what I miss most.

You would always say ours were built the same,

and they are.

Each groove in the knuckle;

each callus on the palm--

Identical.

Yours-- much bigger of course.

mine-- the replica.

Sometimes,

I look down and sob;

droplets falling on my paws,

covering them with salty tears.

It takes me back to the Waves of Sea Isle;

but you aren't there this time,

and I'm not smiling.

I'm standing--

cemented to the ocean floor,

as waves crash through the

e m p t y Void

in my chest.

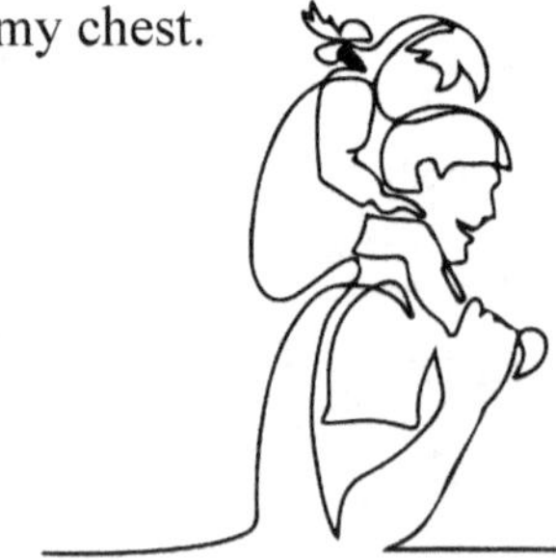

Setting the Bar Low

Your games were *oh* so dignified--
Yahtzee,
Cocaine,
Condemning,
then leaving.

I deserved a
better
fucking,
goodbye.

Pinky Swear

We made so many
promises with our pinkies entwined;
but now-
You use a different finger
every time
you hear
my name.

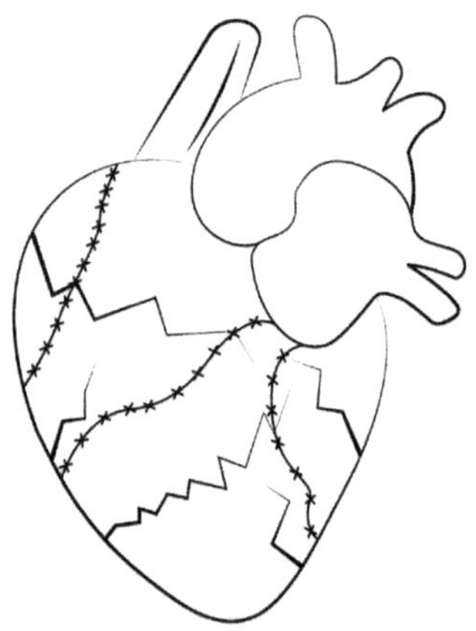

Tatooine Daydreams

Today is your eighth birthday
and I would kill to be there;
looking at your smile
between sticks of laughing fire.

When I last saw you,
we planned the whole thing.
Guest list, party theme,
required costuming.

"Vader" is who you told me
to dress as.
You didn't know then,
that I was already him.

Now I'm alone.
Trapped in the crumbling Death Star.
More machine
than human being.

White helmet,

orange pauldron;

Lightsaber family dinners

we will never have again.

Galaxies of sorrow now

weigh down your shoulders;

gifted to you by damaged adults

who should have known better.

I will forever

be ashamed, regretful,

and entirely sorry--

for being one of them.

Bellies

In the bath water,
I sat in my own filth
writing deep, dark, words-
directed at you.

Twirling bubbles with my foot,
I noticed my toes
looked like tiny people
with red swollen bellies.

Exposed and vulnerable
I realized-
I can't trust
my shoes,
my gut,
or you,

to keep me safe.

My Boat

All this time,

I thought I was waiting

for my ship to come;

but really--

I'm just bit by bit,

recalling a sunken memory

of my life raft leaving,

before

I ever

had a chance,

to get in.

Open Arms

I was never scared of death.
Most of my life
I welcomed it with open arms.
Much like a child does,
to a father who never
wanted them.

Like a recording on repeat,
I say, "Fuck You,"
over and over until I
convince myself
I believe it.

Then, you come back around
and the cycle of torture repeats itself.
"I Love You," "Fuck You."
"I Love You," "Fuck You."

Always spoken with open arms.

Holding Fast?

So why, you ask?

Why do I still care so much?

Care about the accusations?

The interpretations?

My reputation?

Why do I care so much about

People's opinions?

My need to fit in?

A new beginning?

Because I fucking need to.

Pentobarbital

The blood tests didn't matter.
It's Your bones
that got You in the end.

There is no air left in my lungs.
Shallow pants are all that's left-
for both of us.

There are many parts of me
that are crumbling and dying
with You.

Buk's, "Tigers have found me,
and I do not care."

Museum

For I will never be a statue,

not a beacon,

not a mountain top formation.

For I am only an old museum,

filled with mistakes-

nobody needs to pay to see.

Wolves in my Belly

Existence without you is a
hook in my mouth;
cast by God to enslave me.

Shame and self hatred are
worms in my throat;
thrashing in hopes of escaping.

Anxiety and sadness are
crows in my chest;
piercing at grub then receding.

Self-Harm and destruction are
wolves in my belly;
sleeping but softly keep turning.

My steps turn to running
but there's Bombs at my feet;
my whereabouts found by the beeping.

The Beasts have arrived
but never show teeth;
a chase that was never for feeding.

They circle me quickly,
force weight on my body;
"insulation," they say, "for surviving."

Books

People are like books, you know.

Everyone remembers

their first,

their last,

their favorite-

With imprints of their fingerprints

on every page.

Highlighted words of advice

they pledge to live by;

(but never do).

I have spent most of my life,

ashamed of my pages.

My rips,

my wrinkles,

my worn edges.

I kept myself closed so tight;

as to not risk being

marked,

or mocked,

or judged.

I worked so hard trying to

perfect my cover,

that I forgot

the *limitless*

power which I held.

Uncomfortable Silence

Nothing feels right anymore.
like shoes too big,
or gloves too tight.

I sit in complete silence,
brutally biting my nails
down to nothing;

and shred by shred,
I watch every
possibility of happiness,
fall to the ground.

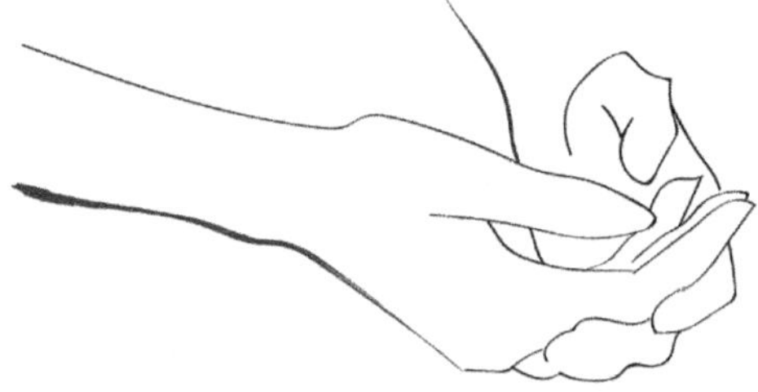

My Peace

Line by line,

calorie by calorie,

mirrors have destroyed

my peace,

my mind.

Little by little,

my soul is dying;

insecurity has destroyed

my peace,

my mind.

The Letter

I coward for mercy,

begging for forgiveness,

after reading your letter

laced with run ons and razor blades.

You said I was a sociopath;

more predatory than anyone

who's ever hurt me.

That cut as deep as you intended.

I was about five years old

When the grooming started.

It lasted as long as my throat

could keep the secret swallowed.

I am more predatory than that man?

I guess then, I deserved it.

Children always do;

don't you think?

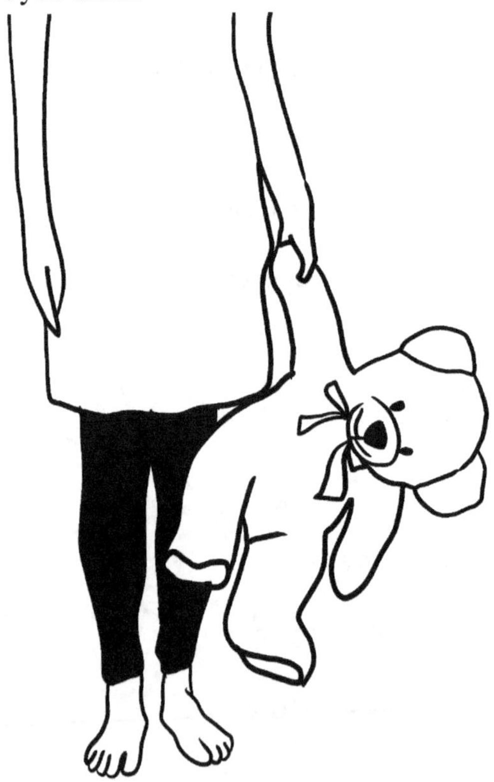

Screaming from the Gallery

Shame! Shame!

I rolled and you floated.

Crossed lines with double vision.

Spilled wine from sacred chalices;

hid the mess under the rug. .

Bang! Bang!

Reality set in quickly.

Jolted us into accessory.

"It must not be so" we shouted;

but the nightmare had just begun.

Shh! Shh!

Secrets birthed left your lips.

Blame was your salvation.

Said you caught the dirty one;

threw stones with no reluctance.

Clang! Clang!

You made sure I was dead.

Put the final nail in my coffin.

Your hammer's very sharp these days;

no silver lining in this story.

Running of the Bulls

Every message I send you
is a white flag,
and your responses-
red.

I'm not sure when you became
the matador,
and I, the bull;

But I foresee myself running for my life
in a frenzied maze,
where you will spear me
to death-
for fun.

Being the Bomb

I've hidden secrets
inside secrets,
wrapped in white lies,
carefully laid in a shallow grave
in the backyard.

I'm paying for sins
piled on sins,
reflected off TV screens.
Breaking my confidence
in an instant.

I'm putting out fires
caught on fire,
trapping energy,
compressed neatly
inside metal.

For a moment I was whole;
for just enough time,

to see myself,

implode on myself-

once again.

I'm sorry to everyone,

for being the bomb.

Watch Me from the Ground

Glorifying attention

I sold my soul;

Broken bones of hope,

(is that all?)

on fabricated affection.

Crazy and destructive;

(self and otherwise).

Donning rose colored glasses,

I drink myself productive.

(Doesn't everyone?)

Cauterizing wounds

(very poorly).

Crashing chemical reactions.

I've survived by bending truths;

(is it working?)

Crumbling reputation;

(I made my bed).

Trading wardrobes with the wolf,

(how do I look?)

lived up to their implications.

Shedding wool coats in waves,

(metaphorically, of course).

collecting jars of moon water;

Trying hard to change.

(For real this time).

Looks of disgust all around;

Blatant objection to my rising;

(fuck you).

You can watch me from the ground.

(How's the view?)

www.ingramcontent.com/pod-product-compliance
Lightning Source LLC
LaVergne TN
LVHW010948200726
843509LV00013B/2328